HOW

Other booklets from *Questions of Life* include:

Christianity: Boring, Untrue or Irrelevant?
How Does God Guide Us?
How and Why Do I Read the Bible?
Does God Heal Today?
Why and How Do I Pray?

Other booklets from *Searching Issues* include:

Why Does God Allow Suffering?
What About Other Religions?
Is There Anything Wrong with Sex Before Marriage?
How Does the New Age Movement Relate to Christianity?
Is the Trinity Unbiblical, Unbelievable and Irrelevant?
Is there a Conflict Between Science and Christianity?
What Is the Christian Attitude to Homosexuality?

How Can I Resist Evil?

NICKY GUMBEL

Alpha

First published 1993 as part of *Questions of Life*
This booklet 2004

Text cartoons by Charlie Mackesy
Cover artwork by Glenn Andrews

ISBN 1 84291 191 0

Published by
KINGSWAY COMMUNICATIONS LTD
Lottbridge Drove, Eastbourne BN23 6NT, England.
Email: books@kingsway.co.uk
Printed in the U.S.A.

Contents

Resisting Evil

There is a close connection between good and God and between evil and the devil. Indeed, in each case the difference is only one letter! Behind the power of good lies Goodness himself. Directly or indirectly behind our own evil desires and the temptations of the world lies evil personified – the devil.

Because there is so much evil in the world some find it easier to believe in the devil than in God. 'As far as God goes, I am a non-believer ... but when it comes to the devil – well that's something else ... the devil keeps advertising ... the devil does lots of commercials,' said William Peter Blatty who wrote and produced *The Exorcist*.[1]

On the other hand, many Westerners find belief in the devil more difficult than belief in God. This may be partly because of a false image of what the devil is like. If the image of God as a white bearded old man sitting on a cloud is absurd and incredible, so also is the image of a horned devil trudging through Dante's inferno. We are not dealing with an alien from outer space but with a real personal force of evil who is active in the world today.

Once we have come to believe in a transcendent God, in some ways it is only logical to accept belief in a devil.

> Belief in a great transcendent power of evil adds nothing whatever to the difficulties imposed by belief in a transcendent power of good. Indeed, it eases them somewhat. For if there were no Satan, it would be hard to resist the conclusion that God is a fiend both because of what he does, in nature, and what he allows, in human wickedness.[2]

According to the biblical worldview behind the evil in the world there lies the devil. The Greek word for the devil, *diabolos*, translates the Hebrew word *satan*. We are not told very much about the origins of Satan in the Bible. There is a hint that he may have been a fallen angel (Isaiah 14:12–23). He appears on a few occasions in the books of the Old Testament (Job 1; 1 Chronicles 21:1). He is not merely a force but is personal.

We are given a clearer picture of his activities in the New Testament. The devil is a personal spiritual being who is in active rebellion against God and has the leadership of many demons like himself. Paul tells us to take our 'stand against the devil's schemes. For our struggle is not against flesh and blood, but against the rulers, against the authorities … against the spiritual forces of evil in the heavenly realms' (Ephesians 6:11–12).

The devil and his angels, according to Paul, are not to be underestimated. They are cunning ('the devil's schemes' v. 11). They are powerful ('rulers', 'authorities' and 'forces' v. 12). They are evil ('forces of evil' v. 12). Therefore, we should not be surprised when we come under a powerful assault from the enemy.

WHY SHOULD WE BELIEVE IN THE DEVIL?

Why should we believe in the existence of the devil? Some say, 'Nowadays you can't believe in the devil.' However, there are very good reasons to believe in his existence.

First, it is biblical. That is not to say that the Bible concentrates on the devil. Satan is not mentioned very often in the Old Testament and it is only when we come to the New Testament that the doctrine is developed more fully. Jesus clearly believed in the existence of Satan and was tempted by him. He frequently cast out demons, freeing people from the forces of evil and sin in their lives, and gave his disciples authority to do the same. In the rest of the New Testament there are many references to the work of the devil (1 Peter 5:8–11; Ephesians 6:1–12).

Secondly, Christians down the ages have almost invariably believed in the existence of the devil. The early church theologians, the Reformers, the great evangelists like Wesley and Whitefield, and the overwhelming majority of men and women of God, knew that there were very real spiritual forces of evil around. As soon as we start to serve the Lord, his interest is aroused. 'The devil only tempts those souls that wish to abandon sin ... the others belong to him: he has no need to tempt them.'[3]

Thirdly, common sense confirms the existence of the devil. Any kind of theology which ignores the existence of a personal devil has a great deal to explain: evil regimes, institutional torture and violence, mass murders, brutal rapes, large scale drug trafficking, terrorist atrocities, sexual and physical abuse of children, occult activity and satanic rituals. Who is behind all of this? There is a ditty which goes like this:

> Some say the devil's been,
> Some say the devil's gone,
> But simple people,
> like you and me,
> Would like to know,
> who carries the business on?

So Scripture, tradition and reason all point to the existence of the devil. This does not mean that we should become obsessed by him. As C. S. Lewis points out, 'There are two equal and opposite errors into which our race can fall about the devils. One is to disbelieve in their existence. The other is to believe, and to feel an excessive and unhealthy interest in them. They themselves are equally pleased by both errors and hail a materialist or a magician with the same delight.'[4]

As Michael Green has put it:

> Like any general who can persuade the opposition to underestimate him, Satan ... must be enchanted at the present state of affairs which leaves him free to operate with the maximum of ease and efficiency, confident that nobody takes him seriously. The more he can do to encourage this doubt of his existence, the better. The more he can blind people's minds to the true state of affairs, the better his aims are furthered.[5]

Many fall into the opposite danger of having an excessive and unhealthy interest in him. There is a whole new interest in spiritualism, palm-reading, ouija boards, 'channelling' (consulting the dead), astrology, horoscopes, witchcraft and occult powers. Involvement in these things is expressly forbidden in Scripture (Deuteronomy 18:10; Leviticus 19:20ff; Galatians

5:19ff; Revelation 21:8; 22:15). If we have meddled in any of these things, we can be forgiven. We need to repent and destroy anything associated with that activity such as books, charms, videos and magazines (Acts 19:19).

Christians too can have an unhealthy interest in these things. A new Christian recently showed me a couple of supposedly Christian books where the whole emphasis was on the work of the enemy – with a lot of space devoted to speculation concerning the number of the beast in Revelation, and tying this in with credit cards! The intention was good, I am sure, but the focus on the work of the enemy seemed to me to be unhealthy. The Bible never has this kind of focus. The spotlight is always on God.

WHAT ARE THE DEVIL'S TACTICS?

The ultimate aim of Satan is to destroy every human being (John 10:10). He wants us to follow a path that leads to destruction. To that end, he tries to prevent anyone coming to faith in Jesus Christ. Paul tells us: 'The god of this age [the devil] has blinded the minds of unbelievers, so that they cannot see the light of the gospel of the glory of Christ, who is the image of God' (2 Corinthians 4:4).

So long as we are going along Satan's path and our eyes are blinded, we will probably be almost totally unaware of his tactics. Once we start walking along the path that leads to life and our eyes are opened to the truth, we become aware that we are under attack.

The initial line of attack is often in the area of doubt. We see this in the opening chapters of Genesis where the enemy, in the form of a serpent, says to Eve, 'Did God *really* say ... ?' His opening move is to raise a doubt in her mind.

We see the same tactic in the temptation of Jesus. The devil comes to him and says, '*If* you are the Son of God …' (Matthew 4:3, italics mine). First, he raises doubts, then come the temptations. His tactics have not changed. He still raises doubts in our mind: 'Did God really say that such and such a course of action is wrong?' or, '*If* you are a Christian … ' He tries to undermine our confidence in what God has said and in our relationship with him. We need to recognise this source of many of our doubts.

Raising doubts was the precursor to the main attack on both Eve in the Garden of Eden and Jesus in the wilderness. In Genesis 3, we see an exposé of the way in which Satan, who is described as 'the tempter' (Matthew 4:2), so often works.

In Genesis 2:16–17, God gave Adam and Eve a far-reaching permission ('You are free to eat from any tree in the garden'), one prohibition ('But you must not eat from the tree of the knowledge of good and evil') and then warned them of the penalty if they disobeyed ('For when you eat of it you will surely die').

Satan ignores the wide scope of the permission and concentrates on the one prohibition – which he then exaggerates (Genesis 3:1). His tactics have not changed. He still ignores the permission. He ignores the fact that God has given us all things richly to enjoy (1 Timothy 6:17). He ignores the great blessing of walking in a relationship with God. He ignores the riches of Christian marriages and families, the security of a Christian home, the level of friendship that we can enjoy as Christians, and countless other things which God offers to those who know and love him. He does not tell us about these things. Instead he concentrates on a tiny unimaginative list of prohibitions of what Christians are not allowed to do – reminding us again and again that we can't get drunk, swear or be promiscuous. There are relatively few things that God does not allow us to do and there are very good reasons why he prohibits them.

Finally, he denies the penalty. He says, 'You will not surely die' (Genesis 3:4). He says, in effect, that it will not do you any harm to disobey God. He suggests to us that God is really a spoilsport, that God does not want the best for our lives and that we will miss out if we don't disobey. In fact the opposite is the case, as Adam and Eve found out. It is disobedience which causes us to miss out on so much of what God intended for us.

In the verses that follow, we see the consequences of disobeying God. First, there is shame and embarrassment. Adam and Eve felt exposed and began a cover-up operation (v. 7). How quickly would we want to leave the room if every action we had ever done was displayed on a screen, followed by a written list of every thought we had ever entertained? Deep down, we all feel ashamed and embarrassed by our sin. We don't want people to find us out. Sir Arthur Conan Doyle once played a practical joke on twelve men. They were all very well-known, respected and respectable men, regarded as pillars of the establishment. He sent each of them a telegram, with the same message in each: 'Flee at once. All is discovered.' Within twenty-four hours, they had all fled the country! Virtually all of us have something in our lives of which we are ashamed; something we would not want everyone to know about. We often put up barriers around us to avoid the possibility of being found out.

Next, Adam and Eve's friendship with God was broken. When they heard God coming, they hid (v. 8). Many people today shy away from God. They don't want to face up to the fact of the possibility of his existence. Like Adam they are afraid

(v. 10). Some have a real fear of going to church or mixing with Christians. A couple in our congregation told me about a sixteen-stone rugby player from Australia whom they had invited to church. He got as far as the drive, then he started shaking in the car. He said, 'I can't go. I'm too frightened to go into the church.' He could not look God in the face. There was a separation between him and God, just as there was with Adam and Eve. God immediately started to try to draw them back into a relationship. He called out, 'Where are you?' (v. 9). He still does.

Then, there is a separation between Adam and Eve themselves. Adam blames Eve. Eve blames the devil. But they and we are responsible for our own sin. We cannot blame God or others or even the devil (James 1:13–15). We see this in our society today. When people turn away from God, they start fighting one another. We see the breakdown of relationships wherever we look: broken marriages, broken homes, broken relationships at work, civil war and war between nations.

Finally, we see in God's punishment of Adam and Eve (v. 14 onwards) that they were deceived by Satan. We see how his deception led Adam and Eve away from God into a path which, as Satan knew from the beginning, led to destruction.

We see that Satan is a deceiver, a destroyer, a tempter and one who raises doubts. He is also an accuser. The Hebrew word for Satan means 'accuser' or 'slanderer'. He accuses God before people. God gets the blame for everything. God, he says, is not to be trusted. Secondly, he accuses Christians before God (Revelation 12:10). He denies the power of the death of Jesus. He condemns us and makes us feel guilty – not for any particular sin, but with a general and vague feeling of guilt. In contrast, when the Holy Spirit draws attention to a sin, he identifies it so that we can turn from it.

Temptation is not the same thing as sin. Sometimes the devil puts a thought into our mind which we know is wrong. At that moment we have a choice whether to accept it or reject it. If we accept it, we are on the way towards sin. If we reject it, we do what Jesus did. He was 'tempted in every way, just as we are – yet was without sin' (Hebrews 4:15). When Satan put evil thoughts in his mind, he rejected them. But often before we have the chance to decide one way or the other, Satan accuses us. Within a split second he says, 'Look at you! Call yourself a Christian? What was that you were thinking about? You can't be a Christian. What a terrible thing to think!' He wants us to agree and say, 'Oh no! I can't be a Christian,' or, 'Oh no! I've blown it now, so it doesn't matter if I blow it a bit more!' We are on the way down, and this is his aim. The tactics are those of condemnation and accusation. If he can provoke guilt in us he knows the thought is: 'It doesn't really make any difference now if I do it or not. I have already failed.' So we do it and temptation becomes sin.

He wants failure to become a pattern in our lives. He knows that the more we fall into sin, the more sin will start to control our lives. The first injection of heroin may not be enough to get a grip, but if you inject it day after day, month after month, year after year, it gets a grip and you become an addict. It has taken hold of you. If we fall into a pattern of doing things which we know to be wrong, these things grip our lives. We become addicted and we are on the path that Satan desires – the one that leads to destruction (Matthew 7:13).

WHAT IS OUR POSITION?

As Christians, God has rescued us from 'the dominion of darkness and brought us into the kingdom of the Son he loves' (Colossians 1:13). Before we were Christians, Paul says, we were in the dominion of darkness. Satan rules us and we were subject to sin, slavery, death and destruction. That is what the dominion of darkness is like.

Now, Paul says, we have been transferred from the kingdom of darkness to the kingdom of light. The moment we come to Christ we are transferred from darkness to light, and in the kingdom of light, Jesus is King. There is forgiveness, freedom, life and salvation. Once we have been transferred, we belong to someone else: to Jesus Christ and his kingdom.

In 1992 the Italian club Lazio paid £5.5 million for Paul Gascoigne to be transferred from Tottenham Hotspur to Lazio. Imagine that Gazza, while playing for Lazio, one day gets a phone-call from Terry Venables, his previous manager at Tottenham Hotspur, saying, 'Why weren't you at the practice this morning?' He would reply, 'I don't work for you any more. I have been transferred. I am working for another club' (or at least that is the gist of what he would say!).

In a far more wonderful way, we have been transferred from the kingdom of darkness where Satan is in charge, to the kingdom of God where Jesus is in charge. When Satan asks us to do his work our reply is, 'I don't belong to you any more.'

Satan is a conquered foe (Luke 10:17–20). On the cross Jesus 'disarmed the powers and authorities' and 'made a public spectacle of them, triumphing over them by the cross' (Colossians 2:15). Satan and all his minions were defeated at the cross, and that is why Satan and his demons are so frightened of the name of Jesus (Acts 16:18). They know they are defeated.

16

Jesus has freed us from guilt, so we don't need to be condemned. He has set us free from addictions. Jesus broke the power of these things and set us free. He broke the fear of death when he defeated death. With that, he set us free, potentially, from every fear. All these things – guilt, addiction and fear – belong to the kingdom of darkness. Jesus has transferred us to a new kingdom.

The cross was a great victory over Satan and his minions, and we now live in the time of the mopping-up operations. Although the enemy is not yet destroyed and is still capable of inflicting casualties, he is disarmed, defeated and demoralised. This is our position, and it is vital to realise the strength of the position we are in, due to the victory of Jesus on the cross for us.

HOW DO WE DEFEND OURSELVES?

Since the war is not over and Satan is not yet destroyed, we need to make sure that our defences are in order. Paul tells us to 'put on the full armour of God so that you can take your stand against the devil's schemes' (Ephesians 6:11). He then mentions six pieces of equipment which we need. Sometimes it is said, 'The secret of the Christian life is … ' But there is no one secret; we need *all* the armour.

First, we need the 'belt of truth' (v. 14). This probably means the foundation of Christian doctrine and truth. It means getting the whole Christian truth (or as much of it as one can) into one's system. We do this by reading the Bible, listening to sermons and talks, reading Christian books and listening to tapes. This will enable us to distinguish what is true and what are Satan's lies, for Satan is 'a liar and the father of lies' (John 8:44).

Next, we need the breastplate of righteousness (v. 14). This is the righteousness that comes from God through what Jesus has done for us on the cross. It enables us to be in a relationship with God and to live a righteous life. We need to resist the devil. The apostle James says, 'Resist the devil, and he will flee from you. Come near to God and he will come near to you' (James 4:7–8). We all fall from time to time. When we do, we need to get up quickly. We do this by telling God how sorry we are for what we have done, being as specific as possible (1 John 1:9). He then promises to restore his friendship with us.

Then, we also need the boots of the gospel of peace (v. 15). I understand this to mean a readiness to speak about the gospel of Jesus Christ. As John Wimber often said, 'It is hard to sit still and be good.' If we are constantly seeking opportunities to pass on the good news, we have an effective defence against the enemy. Once we declare our Christian faith to our families and at work, we strengthen our defence. It is hard, because we know that we are being watched to see if we live up to our faith. But it is a great incentive to do so.

The fourth piece of armour is the shield of faith (v. 16). With this, we 'can extinguish all the flaming arrows of the evil one'. Faith is the opposite of cynicism and scepticism which wreak havoc in many lives. One aspect of faith has been defined as 'taking a promise of God and daring to believe it'. Satan will throw his arrows of doubt to undermine us – but with the shield of faith we resist him.

Fifthly, Paul tells us to take the helmet of salvation (v. 17). As Bishop Westcott, Regius Professor of Divinity at Cambridge, once pointed out, there are three tenses of salvation. We have been saved from the penalty of sin. We are being saved from the power of sin. We shall be saved from the presence of sin. We need to grasp these great concepts in our mind; to know them so that we can answer the enemy's doubts and accusations.

Finally, we are to take 'the sword of the Spirit, which is the word of God' (v. 17). Probably here Paul is thinking of the Scriptures. Jesus used the Scriptures when Satan attacked. Each time Jesus replied with the word of God and in the end Satan had to leave. It is well worth learning verses from the Bible which we can use to see off the enemy and remind ourselves of the promises of God.

HOW DO WE ATTACK?

As we have already seen, Satan and his minions were defeated on the cross, and we are now involved in the final mopping-up operations before the return of Jesus. As Christians, we need not be afraid of Satan; he has a great deal to fear from the activity of Christians.

We are called to pray. We are involved in spiritual warfare, though 'the weapons we fight with are not the weapons of the world. On the contrary, they have divine power to demolish strongholds' (2 Corinthians 10:4). Prayer was a very high priority for Jesus, and it should be for us. In the words of the hymn, 'Satan trembles when he sees the weakest Christian on his knees.'

We are also called to action. Again, in the life of Jesus, prayer and action go hand in hand. Jesus proclaimed the kingdom of God, healed the sick and cast out demons. He commissioned his disciples to do the same.

It is important to stress the greatness of God and the relative powerlessness of the enemy. We do not believe that there are two equal and opposite powers – God and Satan. That is not the biblical picture. God is the Creator of the universe. Satan is a part of his creation – a fallen part. He is a small part. Further, he is a defeated enemy and is about to be utterly wiped out when Jesus returns (Revelation 12:12).

In a superb picture in C. S. Lewis' book *The Great Divorce*, where he speaks about hell as the place where Satan and his demons operate, a man has arrived in heaven and is being shown round by his 'teacher'. He goes down on hands and knees, takes a blade of grass and, using the thin end as a pointer, he eventually finds a tiny crack in the soil in which is concealed the whole of hell:

'Do you mean then that Hell – all that infinite empty town – is down in some little crack like this?'

'Yes. All Hell is smaller than one pebble of your earthly world: but it is smaller than one atom of *this* world, the Real World. Look at yon butterfly. If it swallowed all Hell, Hell would not be big enough to do it any harm or to have any taste.'

'It seems big enough when you are in it, Sir.'

'And yet all loneliness, angers, hatreds, envies and itchings that it contains, if rolled into one single experience and put into the scale against the least moment of the joy that is felt by the least in Heaven, would have no weight that could be registered at all. Bad cannot succeed even in being bad as truly as good is good. If all Hell's miseries together entered the consciousness of yon wee yellow bird on the bough there, they would be swallowed up without trace, as if one drop of ink had been dropped into that Great Ocean to which your terrestrial Pacific itself is only a molecule.'[6]

Notes

1. Alan MacDonald, *Films in Close Up* (Frameworks, 1991).
2. Michael Green, *I Believe in Satan's Downfall* (Hodder & Stoughton, 1981).
3. Jean-Baptiste Vianney.
4 C. S. Lewis, *The Screwtape Letters* (Fount, 1942).
5. Michael Green, *I Believe in Satan's Downfall*.
6. C. S. Lewis, *The Great Divorce* (Fount, 1973).

Study Guide

1. Why do you think *'many westerners find belief in the devil more difficult than belief in God'* (p. 7)?
2. What dangers are there in *'an excessive and unhealthy interest'* in devils (p. 10)?
3. What tactics does the devil use in an individual's life (p. 11.)?
4. What is the difference between temptation to sin and sin itself (p. 15.)? Why is this distinction so important?
5. How does our relationship to the devil change when we become Christians (p. 16.)? What are the practical consequences of this?
6. In Ephesians 6 Paul mentions six pieces of the Christian's *'armour'*. What do you think each of these means in practice?
7. In what ways are we called upon to be involved in the spiritual warfare between good and evil (p. 19.)?

Alpha

This book is an Alpha resource. The Alpha course is a practical introduction to the Christian faith initiated by Holy Trinity Brompton in London, and now being run by thousands of churches throughout the UK as well as overseas.

For more information on Alpha, and details of tapes, videos and training manuals, contact the Alpha office, Holy Trinity Brompton on 0207 581 8255, (home page: http://www.alphacourse.org), or STL, PO Box 300, Kingstown Broadway, Carlisle, Cumbria CA3 0QS.

Alpha Hotline for telephone orders:
0845 7581 278 (all calls at local rate)

To order from overseas:
Tel +44 1228 611749
Fax +44 1228 514949

Email: alpha@stl.org

Alpha

Alpha titles available

Alpha: Questions of Life   The Alpha course in book form. In fifteen compelling chapters Nicky Gumbel points the way to an authentic Christianity which is exciting and relevant to todays world.

Searching Issues   The seven issues most often raised by participants on the Alpha course: suffering, other religions, sex before marriage, the New Age, homosexuality, science and Christianity, and the Trinity. Also available as booklets.

A Life Worth Living   What happens after Alpha? Based on the book of Philippians, this is an invaluable next step for those who have just completed the Alpha course, and for anyone eager to put their faith on a firm biblical footing.

How to Run the Alpha Course: Telling Others   The theological principles and the practical details of how courses are run. Each alternate chapter consists of a testimony of someone whose life has been changed by God through an Alpha course.

Challenging Lifestyle   Studies in the Sermon on the Mount showing how Jesus' teaching flies in the face of modern lifestyle and presents us with a radical alternative.

The Heart of Revival   Ten Bible studies based on the book of Isaiah, drawing out important truths for today by interpreting some of the teaching of the Old Testament prophet Isaiah. The book seeks to understand what revival might mean and how we can prepare to be part of it.

30 Days   Nicky Gumbel selects thirty passages from the Old and New Testament which can be read over thirty days. It is designed for those on an Alpha course and others who are interested in beginning to explore the Bible.

Why Jesus?   A booklet – given to all participants at the start of the Alpha course. 'The clearest, best illustrated and most challenging short presentation of Jesus that I know.' – Michael Green

*All titles are by Nicky Gumbel, who is on the staff of
Holy Trinity Brompton*